eteam

BUZZ CUT

This book was published with support by *UCR ARTSblock* in conjunction with the exhibition: *Free Enterprise, The Art of Citizen Space Exploration* at the Culver Center of the Arts & Sweeney Art Gallery and the California Museum of Photography. January - May 2013.

The exhibition was organized by Tyler Stallings and Marko Peljahn. *Buzz Cut* is a companion to eteam's two channel video installation: *The backup tapes from Moon and Mars,* commissioned by UCR ARTSblock *for Mara Miranda and Louis Leopold*

We return in October. This time we fly. We approach Moon from above and touch ground with a delay of about one hour in the evening of October 11, 2012. In the underground garage we strap a seat and a child into the back of a silver Chrysler 300S and drive for 10 minutes along an empty highway through the even distribution of shiny raindrops until we reach our motel, America's Best Value Inn, 8858 University Blvd, Moon. Everything is dark, except the illuminated box that hangs above the short staircase. It spells out the word LOBBY in black on white light, as if it was the title sequence for a film noir. That is it for the night. A structure with a roof, three rusty stories old, rooms with strangers in beds, tiled bathrooms, black TVs, and a bible in the drawer of every nightstand.

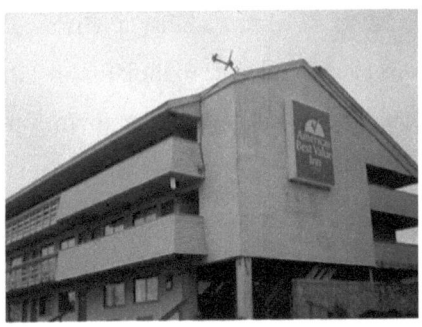

The next morning when we appear in the lobby, we have already missed breakfast. An attendant in a white shirt and a beige tie pops up from behind a counter and delivers the news without any signs of emotion. "The times that are printed on the card have changed," he says. "Overnight?" we ask, but he has already submerged back into the vacuum zone behind the desk that does not provide enough oxygen for conversations. We walk into the breakfast room and take a look.

Eight clumsy chairs are upside down on two tables, sticking their stiff legs into the thin air like electrocuted insects. There is a stack of translucent plastic containers on an oversized kitchen counter, partially covering the sink, which hadn't been removed when one of the guest rooms was converted into the motel's breakfast room. Next to the stack sits a black thermos for coffee, a black thermos for hot water, and a quietly vibrating machine with a metal facade from which one could choose three different kinds of sugared juices, if only there were cups.

We leave with the feeling of having missed out on something and get into the car. "The Moon is a harsh Mistress," Robert A. Heinlein wrote, in 1966. We decide to look for breakfast in Mars.

We know our way from Moon, the township along the Ohio River in Allegheny Country, Pennsylvania, USA, population 24,185, to Mars, the borough in Butler County, Pennsylvania, USA, population 1,746. While it may take six months to cover that distance with a rocket in extraterrestrial space, it only takes 40 minutes in the simulation. We head northeast on University Blvd. and continue onto PA-51. The navigator of the on-board entertainment system suggests a different route, but we decline. We know better. We have memories. We take the small bridge that leads us onto Neville Island, in the middle of the Ohio River. On the island, we drive down Grand Avenue until we get to the shiny white Neville Island bridge, which carries I-79 across the second half of the Ohio River. Eventually, we take exit 78 towards Mars. Before crossing the border into Mars we stop in the parking lot of the last chain store on Earth.

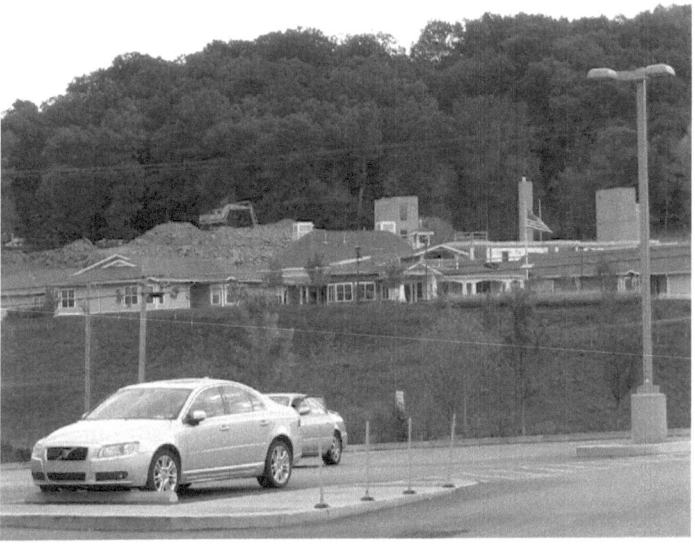

We get out of the car and look at two yellow Caterpillar backhoes in the hills that tower above the slightly tilted roofs of newly built houses. They are all still. Not a single überarm pumps its hydraulic muscles to scoop up the dirt. There is not even dust in the air. We enter the store. It's bright in there, warm and dry, devoid of people. We walk through colorful aisles of fully stocked shelves towards the back, where a middle-aged human in a white lab coat sorts white plastic bottles into drawers behind a cutout window in the wall. He is too immersed in his routine to notice we are there. We turn around, find different kinds of clear water in aisle twenty-three, take two bottles of the cheapest brand, that supposedly comes out of the Earth in a spring, and stroll back towards the cashier, wondering what else we could buy, since we are here anyway. Nothing catches our interest. The cashier station is abandoned. We shout out a "Hello" two or three times until an elderly woman in dark green sweatpants and a burgundy company coat materializes on top of the industrial carpet near a door with a red glowing emergency exit sign. She approaches the cashier station slowly, like a caterpillar, lifting and compressing her upper body with each tiny step. She grabs the scanner pistol with all ten fingers and scans the price tags of our water bottles. When the price appears on the LED screen, we take a sensor card out of our wallet and hold it in midair until she points into the direction of the card reader and makes a swiping gesture, her chin down, as if someone might punch her at any moment. We swipe the card and the receipt starts printing; when it is done, she rips the paper from the roll and pushes it flat over the counter. We take it and leave the store without having ever looked into her eyes.

Five minutes later we are in the center of Mars, next to a piece of green lawn with a silver saucer, cornered by the Mars Brew House and the side wall of Barbieri's Barber Styling Shop. The windowless side wall is covered with plastic strips of white vinyl siding. The only interruption in the even whiteness is a barber pole with a helix of blue, red, and white, continuously revolving in the upper right corner of the façade. We've always wondered why barbers use this kind of symbol and look it up on our smart device.

During medieval times, barbers did all kinds of things. They cut hair, shaved beards, they performed head surgeries and extracted teeth. Next to each barber chair was a staff that patients gripped during either one of these procedures to deal with the pain. The red stripes represent bloody bandages wrapped around a pole. Because barbers were also in the business of bloodletting, the typical pole in a barber shop had also two brass wash basins, one at the top, where they kept the leeches, and one at the bottom, where they collected the customer's blood. In this case the pole was for patients to grip during bloodletting, to encourage the flow of blood.

We walk around the side towards the front of the building that faces Grand Avenue. E.T. sits in the window on a child's bicycle, next to a green alien in a black T-shirt. When we open the door, the frame pushes a metal bell that rings.

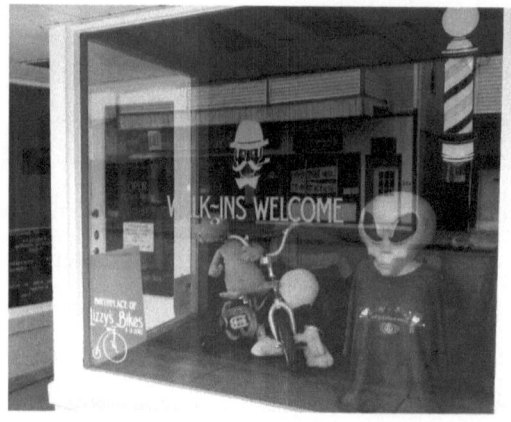

Two barbers are stationed in front of a mirrored wall, behind revolving chairs covered by red-and-white-striped teepees. On top of each tent sits a grinning human head. One barber greets us with an enthusiastic "Hello, we know you!" and then returns to shaving the hair off the head in front of him with an electrical razor. The other barber just smiles. We receive no instructions, so we sit down on the raw green foam of a waiting bench that looks like exposed stalagmites at the bottom of a cave. Then we watch, then we wait, then we relax and listen to the music on the radio. About 30 minutes and two head shavings later, the barber with the black-and-white Three Stooges tie, who works closer to the window, says we should come back tomorrow and talk to his brother. Tomorrow would be a better time. We knew it.

Back on Grand Avenue we pull out the stack of dialogues and quotes we had prepared for people to say, in case nobody would talk to us. We skim through the options and look around.

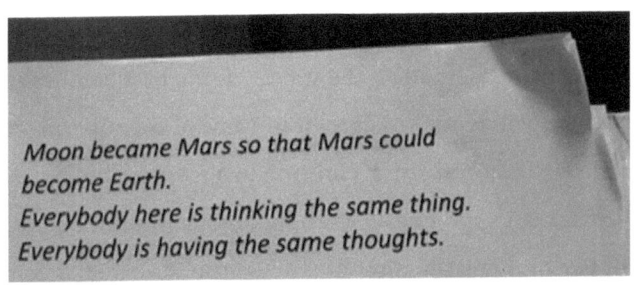

Moon became Mars so that Mars could become Earth.
Everybody here is thinking the same thing.
Everybody is having the same thoughts.

Whom to ask? Right next to Barbieri's Barber Styling Shop is the Mars Travel Agency. We try the door, but it is locked. We press our heads against the glass front and wait as our eyes adjust to see the dark side of a galactic travel business. On one side there is a brown desk with a black leather chair; on the other, two generic armchairs. Brittle wings from out-of-business airlines hang from the ceiling on translucent fishing line. There is an old globe that shows what would happen if the Earth stopped rotating around itself. North and South America in the middle latitudes are almost gone, bleached out by the sun. There is a cutout of a palm tree on a sandy cardboard beach, a dusty model of a grey cruise liner, and a flat, stiff, smiling stewardess. These are the highlights. The rest is brown carpet with a couple of stains, dark wood paneling, chest-high fire-resistant metal filing cabinets, wastebaskets woven out of withered palm leaves, and an ancient computer screen salvaged from an Egyptian pyramid. The windowsill is covered with tall stacks of glossy cruise vacation catalogs and small stacks of business cards that promote the agency's motto: "From Mars to

Moon into the World." Moon has the airport in the region.

We keep walking down the street, passing by a handwritten fluorescent orange super sale sign in front of the supermarket, and enter the bakery in a cute white Victorian house, with black trimmings and purple lavender bushes around the porch. It's a busy time for the tiny shop. The air is saturated with the molecules of powdered sugar that periodically emit from the back room. A white marbled counter divides the room in half. It is intensely stacked with sugared goods on silver trays and cake stands. There is enough metal and harsh icing to make the presentation look like a recycling station for crashed cars, squeezed in between a lemon-walled shopping mall and a marzipan-covered daycare center— a little bit out of this world.

Behind the counter stands a female crane in a pink apron. She has brought her arm into position to maneuver the sugared goods into paper bags and cardboard boxes, but her preparedness keeps getting undermined. The three mothers with accompanying children who she is paid to serve can't decide what they want, and while they discuss their options we take in the rest of the shop's decoration. The theme is overindulgence made look pretty decadent. There is no concept of moderation. Everything exists in the extreme, is bigger, sweeter, gooier and loaded with chunks of candy bars, roasted marshmallows and genetically modified nuts. The wall across the entrance is covered with glossy coffee table books that feature chocolate cakes in the shape of hats worn by the police in England, Russia, or Morocco, along with cupcakes that look like broccoli. A triangular corner accent table is used to present locally sewn aprons and potholders, next to candy bags with metal-wired ribbons that continuously fly up into the air, forecasting the times when gravity won't be an issue any longer. There are pizza-sized multi-swirled lollipops on plastic sticks, caramel-coated baby dolls, and crystal-crusted rocks that cause nasty tooth decay. The crane is beginning to look stressed. Her arm has sagged down to the position of a closed railway crossing gate, while her eyes have turned into red flashing lights. The counter has turned into a roadblock, and the three women and their small children are in a state of emergency. Two of the kids are kicking the counter, while the others are still arguing which mini cupcakes should be rescued first from the pressuring mountains of cold and unforgiving frosting. The second, much older group of women in the store start making their voices heard. "I take one, you take one, and she takes one." They all will eat one of the potato chip cookies the bakery is famous for. "One for each of us!" they shout, and swing their dollar bills through the air like picket signs. But it's not their turn yet. The crane works by the rules. This delays the anticipated sugar shock. Their voices grow louder. Their cheeks turn red, and one of them starts producing an intense-smelling armpit sweat that doesn't mix well with the acrylic fibers of her red fleece shirt.

We don't feel like asking anyone to choose a dialogue from our folder and read it aloud. This is not the place to talk about comparative planetology, not the time to sketch out the difference between living in the simulation of Mars and Moon as a preparation for expansion of human life into outer space. We don't want to know anything, Captain William had said on his first and last expedition to Mars, pouting out his thick lips. "We already know it."

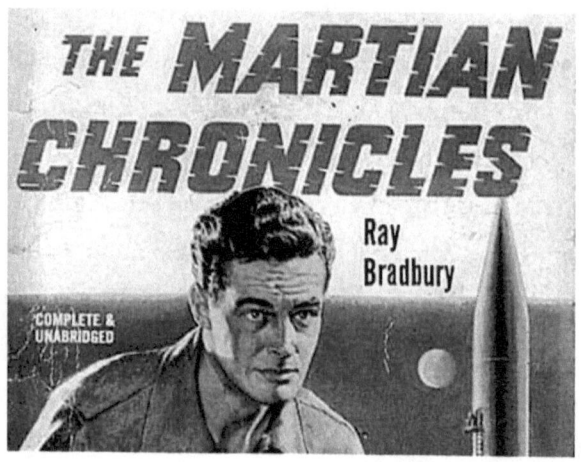

We stumble back onto the street and find relief in the library. There is a big sofa with a view of a wall filled with books. On top of it hangs a metal sign that says: FICTION. We sit down and relax. Fiction is always an option. After a while a librarian with cute over-the-nose rimmed glasses approaches and asks if we need help in finding anything. We ask her about the big black telescope. "What do people do with it?"

"They read the sky", she says, sticking with the vocabulary of a librarian to describe what an astronomer would probably call a different thing. She does not seem in a hurry, so we keep rephrasing our question, each time becoming a little bit more suggestive. We want her to confirm that people actually seldom check out the telescope,

For looking back would have been sickening to the heart.

We look at the books and start drifting away. We are beyond. We are lonely. We are not lost, but we are lonely. The librarian should talk about these things. She should tell us how it feels. The universe is dark and endless. What are the chances our paths will cross again? We reach out to touch her hand, but there is no hand. There is only her short brown hair and that amazing paleness in her face, which looks like a fat-free stick of butter in a refrigerator the head of a family buys in bulk every first Friday of the month in a discount wholesale center. We want her to warm up and tell us about her house, her days, her nights, her bedroom, and the plastic globe on her nightstand, but she refuses and says she has no globe at home. We want her to melt—just for the heck of it, want her to admit that there hasn't been a night in many years when she could fall asleep without turning on the light inside the globe and letting her fingers run over the warm, elevated sections of the continents, the valleys, the poles, the peaks, Mount McKinley,

Mount Massive, Mount Harvard, Mount Princeton, Grizzly Peak, Pilot Peak, while she is crying without sound and tears.

The words don't escape her mouth. Instead she chooses the more conservative option, and explains the procedure of filling out an application to become a member of the Mars library.

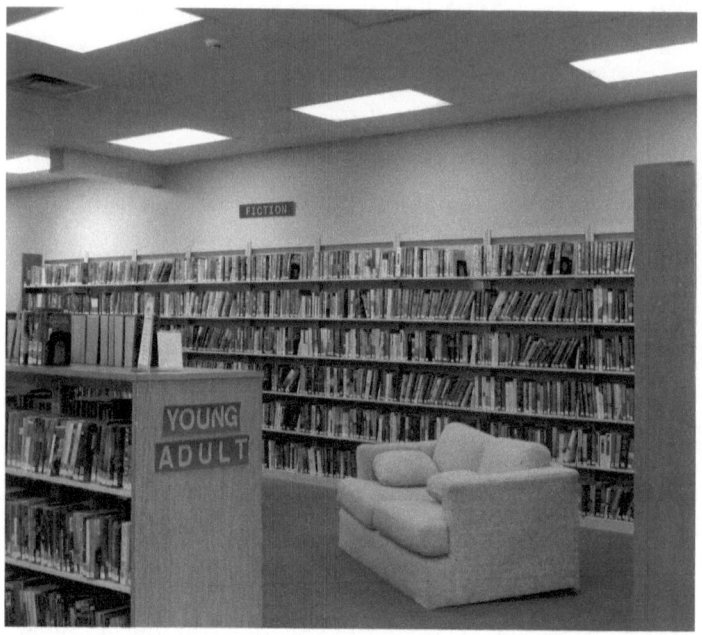

The last non-residential building on Grand Avenue is a kind of farm store, where a man and his two sons sell different kinds of gravel to cover their neighbor's front yards when they're too hard to mow. We take a close-up picture of each of the gravel patches on display and then walk back towards the Mars National Bank, where we spontaneously wave at a handsome bank teller through the window. This kind of thing always pays off. We swing around and face the village green with new energy. It's unclear why we have never before noticed the old-fashioned clock next to the silver saucer. We cross the street to get a closer look. It's five minutes to noon and the big handle keeps ticking forward. A woman walks by and says that she had never seen this chronometer before. It's it almost predictable now that this must mean something. That time will tell, that this clock tries to communicate the same story as the clock on top of our vehicle's board computer and the clock in one of the new developments.

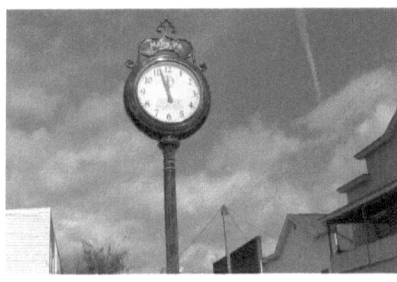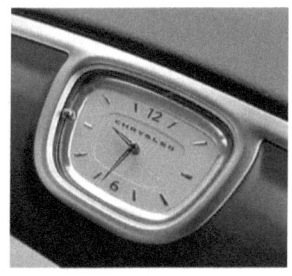

Everything counts. A leaf on the ground could contain as much information as a bag full of garbage. Evidence is faithful. It includes everything that is used to reveal the truth. The facts are all there, all laid out in front of us. But it is impossible to collect them. We start to select, to determine what qualifies as evidence, and that's when the bigger picture starts to escape us. When we decide what to bring forward and what to leave behind.

The ship's bell, cemented onto a thick concrete pedestal next to the silver saucer, looks as if she is ready to reveal some important history. We bang on her sturdy shell with a certain degree of respect. The bell vibrates deeply and hums elongated sound waves. As the waves start to disappear into the atmosphere, we press our ears on her cold body, feeling, rather than hearing, as the remaining waves struggle to escape. When they are gone, we bang again, and that's when they are telling us that this is the same ancient voice that Mister K. heard when he sat in his room

reading from a metal book with raised hieroglyphs over which he brushed his hand, as one might play a harp. And from the book, as his fingers stroked, a voice sang, a soft ancient voice, which told tales of when the sea was red steam on the shore and ancient men had carried clouds of metal insects and electric spiders into battle.

The little boy isn't interested in listening. He runs through the wet grass and then onto the sidewalk where the prints of his rubber-soled shoes press themselves onto the dry concrete. The print is only visible for a few seconds before it dissolves into nothing. We ask him to run through the grass and then over the test field again. Then again—to measure the time it takes for that kind of evidence to be erased—before we walk down Marshall Way and cross the ancient railroad tracks that approach the flat horizon with the straightforwardness of a mystery novel. In the end, there will be a conclusion.

Timothy and Michael and Robert and Mom
and Dad.
    The Martians stared back up at them for a long, long
silent time from the rippling water. . . .

We look at the railroad. If nothing else comes up, we will have to follow these tracks and look at the relics of the Mars Station, the place where it all started in 1875, but for now we hope to skip the history lesson. What we want is an idea of the future. Behind the tracks is the Mars Animal Depot, and across from it a big pile of raw soil from Earth that hides a white church from heaven.

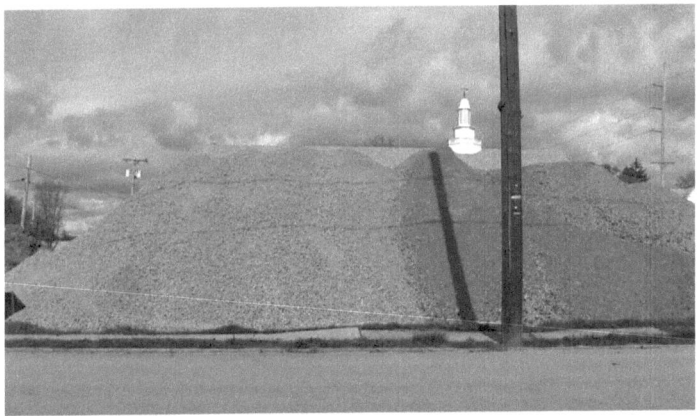

The light changes rapidly and the clouds cast fast-moving shadows, until they are suddenly all gone and the sky turns into

the blue sky of Mars as if it might at any
moment grip in on itself, contract, and expel a shining
miracle down upon the sand.

Nothing happens, even though something was going to happen. If this is the place, it's not the time. We turn around and look at the leaves on the tree that will fall off within the next two days. They are brown and they are rattling and they are falling. They know, we know, everybody knows. It's fall time.

The ground below the tree is covered with rocks. They are smaller than apples but bigger than walnuts, and partially covered by the withered leaves that have already separated from the tree. We are not quite ready, yet, to understand that this is not a preview of what is going to happen. We need to get initiated first. We need to receive a simple sign and then take it from there. Something like a door.

We take cover behind the tree and focus on the door of Mars Animal Depot that leads to the parking lot. It opens, and a middle-aged couple steps out into the wind. The man carries a big dead dog in his arms. He is followed by a woman, who carries a flabby, brown, blanket. They open the trunk of a car, put the dead dog in, lay the blanket on top and close it softly, like a casket. Then they drive away. We wait. A white truck pulls up and parks next to the spot the dead dog's car had just occupied. The printing on the side says: Stericycle. Protecting People. Reducing Risk. Infectious/Chemotherapeutic Waste. PA- HC0196.

The driver gets out and walks into the Animal Depot through the same door the couple had just used to carry out

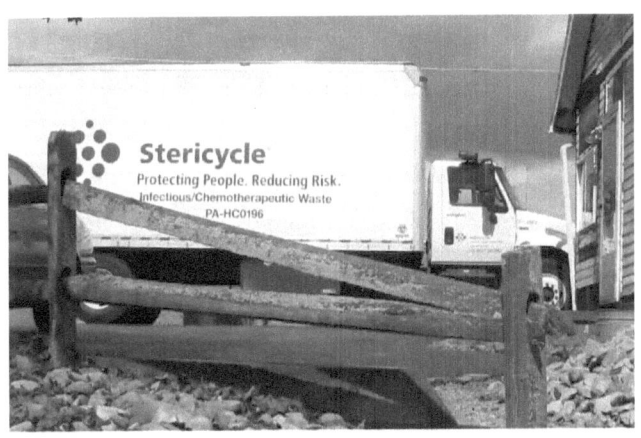

their dead companion. We feel a small rush of adrenaline. Something is happening. The driver comes out again. He carries two white containers, puts them in the back of the truck, climbs into the cabin, and drives off. That was good, we think. Very good, we say, and look again at the stones covering the ground. Most of them are grey. Some are black, some are white, some are smooth, some are rough. A few have more holes than mass. They look like frozen lava. Eventually cluster genealogists will see our ancestor's skulls in them.

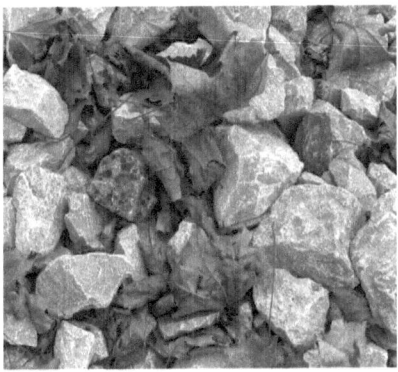

The little boy sits on the ground and breaks branches from the tree into pieces. While we were watching the door, he has sorted through the rocks and lined a few of them up in a row. The display looks as convincing as an exhibit in a museum, but without the tags that state the age and the weight and the name of the matter, there is no proof of anything. We start scanning the horizon for more obvious signs, hoping this thing would occur this thing expected all day, this thing that could not occur but might.

Wooden poles are evenly spaced out along the sidewalk across the street, elevating an electrical power line. In the middle between two of them, a piece of wood has grown around the cable, yet there is no sign that there has ever been a tree on that site.

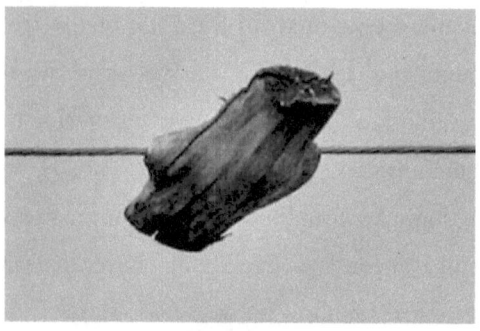

We keep moving forward and scan the ground on Marshall Way across from the Mars National Bank, where the outer part of the sidewalk is covered with iron saturated bricks that have names, years, or planets with planetary ring systems embossed into them. We assume the bricks with a name and only one number refer to people still living, and that the bricks with a name and two numbers refer to the departed. Thomas J. Beidl,

1955—1980. He must have been only 25 years old when he left Earth. Every fact comes with a certain amount of sadness. Once in a while, the only way to deal with it is to put a brick in front of the Mars National Bank, or to install a white pole next to a silver fir tree and a saucer on the lawn of the village green. In actuality, the pole is nothing else but an eight-foot high 4x4 piece of wood, painted white. The side facing the street says: "May Peace prevail on Earth" in the most widely used language on Earth. The other three sides carry the same message in French, Russian, and Spanish. The pole has power. Every time we get close to it, the whole universe turns into a tiny green lawn and all we can think of is: "May piece prevail on Earth".

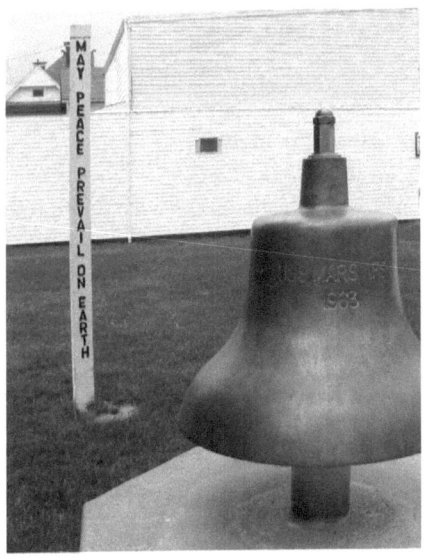

There is no point in getting sentimental before breakfast. Suzie Q's across the street is closed. There is a handwritten sign behind the glass of the entrance that says: We are out of power.

Our second choice is Jimmy's Grille. It's the place with the most square footage and the highest amount of framed photographs in town. One can also eat there. In August, during the preliminaries, we sat in the booth next to the triple-life-size portrait of a big smiling girl. The words printed underneath her round white chin explained that she was gone, that her condition had taken her body away, but that memories of her would always being kept alive by her parents, who appeared to be the owners of the restaurant.

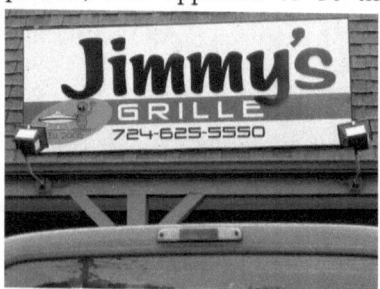

It takes two minutes to drive there. We park the car right in front of the door, lock it, and approach the entrance door with a strange feeling in the Adam's apple. It is as if we are about to meet an old acquaintance again. We open the door and there she is. Triple life sized. We nod into the direction of the dead smiling girl and sit as far away from her as possible, in order to communicate with the location's memory from a different vantage point. Our instinct is rewarded. We get transported instantly, as the simulated reality of an antique town square wraps itself around us without any effort. That's where we want to be.

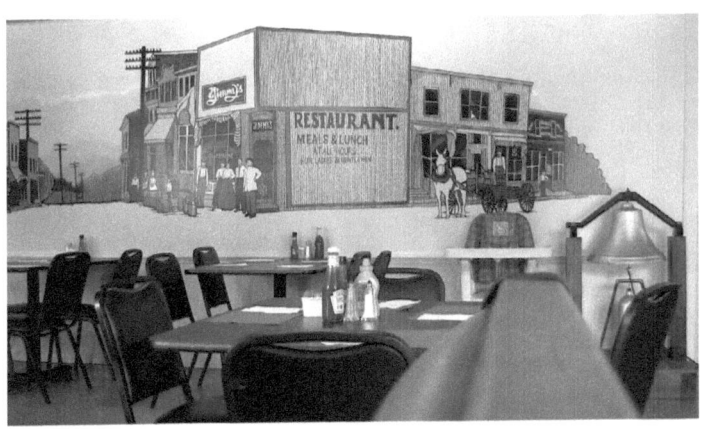

It takes a while, but eventually the waiter enters the picture. He is tall and long-limbed, dressed completely in black and hunched over. He is in a rush, even though there are only three other customers in the whole place. We order the same dishes we ordered last time, when the same waiter had been dressed in black, hunched over and been in a rush. Three fish filets with tartar sauce and two regular teas in black cups with a slice of yellow lemon.

Our consultation with Irene is at 3pm the next day. Her office is in the basement of the Mars Professional Building. We knock on her door at 2:55pm. She opens promptly, smiles and gives us a hug as soft and pleasant as a flower on a jasmine bush.

We talk a while about the child and then she turns off the fluorescent light. We set up our audio recorder and settle down in the woven chairs in the corner of the room. Irene is only three feet across from us; our knees are almost touching, but not quite yet.

"Talk to me," Irene says quietly, with a pleasant smile.

We tell Irene that we thought about what she told us last time, that Mars in astrology is the planet of energy, action, and desire, that Mars is male, that Mars is the surviving force in us, that it rules our animal instincts for aggression, anger, and survival. Mars is direct, we say, Mars is basic. With Mars there is no contemplation before action. Irene nods, but she doesn't say anything. We look at our notes. Last time Irene told us we should look at Mars from above, that we should think about the term Ancient. We did more research on that," we tell her. "We looked at satellite images of Mars.

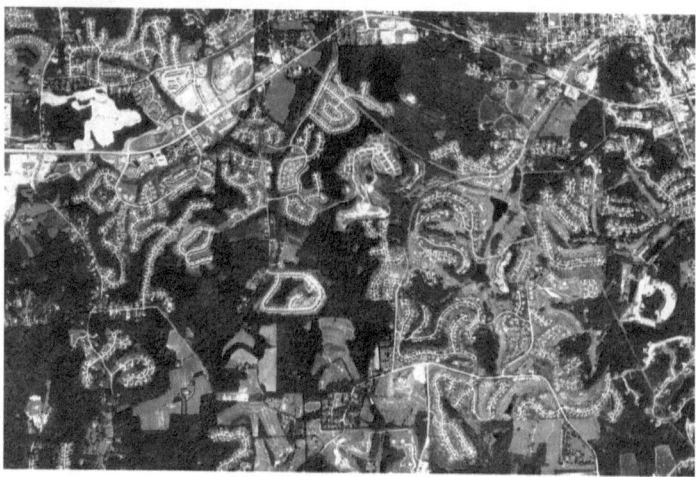

We started in the center and then we branched out and looked at the new developments. The layout reminded us of ferns, and then of fern fossils and petrified fronds unfurling. Then one thing led to another, and we got from people selling titanic chunks of Pennsylvanian fern fossils on eBay to lichens. Lichens, we found out, are symbiotic creatures. They are not a single organism, but a result of a partnership between a fungus and a photosynthetic partner. They occur everywhere, even in the most extreme environments on earth, and they grow very slowly. Some of them are 1000s of years old and there is one species that's called map lichen."

In 2008 map lichen had been sent to outer space, where they were exposed to space conditions for 15 days before being brought back down to earth, where they showed 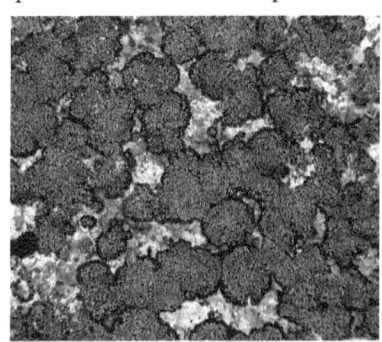 minimal changes or damage. They are extremely resistant to the harsh environment of outer space."

Irene stares at us. Her upper body rests against the back of the chair. Her hands lie on the armrests, both of her feet are touching the ground. She keeps breathing evenly and then says:

"Thank you for sharing that with me, because I don't remember what I say when I am in an alternate state. Is there anything else you want to share before I connect?"

"Someone in Mars has mowed crop circles into a field," we say. We tell Irene that yesterday we went to that place, that we drove up the driveway and knocked on the door of the house that was closest to where the figure had been mowed

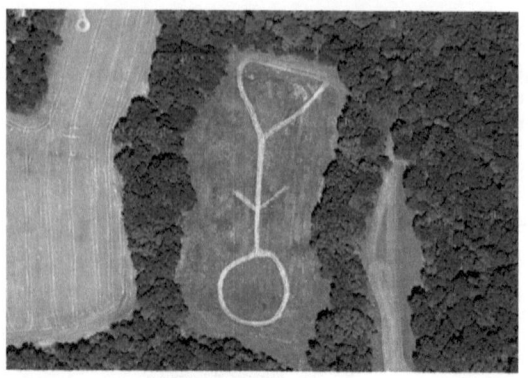

into the field. And that an old woman had opened the door. She held a feverish child in her arms. She said her son had mowed the figure into the field, but that he was out of town. We ask Irene: "Is that something that relates to the ancient?" Irene stares at us, and then swallows what we have told her. Then she smiles.

"Magicians, sorcerers," whispered one of the Earth Men.
"No, hallucination. They pass their insanity over into us so that we see their hallucinations too. Telepathy. Autosuggestion and telepathy."

She closes her eyes and takes a deep breath. Her hands are now resting in her lap with the palms turned towards the plastic tiles on the low ceiling of the basement. She keeps breathing in and out very deeply, and answers with her eyes closed. The information arrives in soft waves.

"You've been asking about the developments", Irene says, "and they want you to know…. that the area emerged as a simulation. A couple of years ago special tax breaks started smashing down like … meteorites, and led to massive re-shaping. I am hearing … it was a hypothetical process … of deliberately modifying the atmosphere, temperature, surface topography, and ecology in order to make it habitable by humans. The tax breaks were meant … to encourage growth … and they worked. Mars had always been the most likely candidate for terraforming … but I am also hearing … it was not as formally structured … or intelligently designed that way. It's just happening as if you … put grains of sand on the head of a drum … and you put on a certain sound of music … how these grains of sand will form a certain pattern … they are saying that's how this residential area was formed … Not because there was a conscious awareness of our connection … it's more subconscious … is what I am getting. People don't realize why they are here and yet … there is a correlation."

It was coming nearer.
At any moment it might happen.
It was like those days when you heard a thunderstorm coming and there was the waiting silence and then the faintest pressure of the atmosphere as the climate blew over the land in shifts and shadows and vapors. And the change pressed at your ears and you were suspended in the waiting time of the coming storm. You began to tremble. The sky was stained and colored; the clouds were thickened; the mountains took on an iron taint. The caged flowers blew with faint sighs of warning. You felt your hair stir softly. Somewhere in the house the voice-clock sang, "Time, time, time, time . . ."

We are back on the street, on top of the hill next to the church. We take a deep breath and connect. This is the town of Mars. It's as simple as that. Leaves are blowing down the sidewalks, a flag is waving in the wind, and people are walking in and out of the post office with silver keys in their hands. Written communication in downtown Mars is routed through one central hub, and each resident within the zip code of 16046 has access to written correspondence and paper bills through a small metal door with a number, as long as they physically submit themselves to walk down the postal path. We wait for further clarification. At 3:45pm, when the lighting is right, it starts.

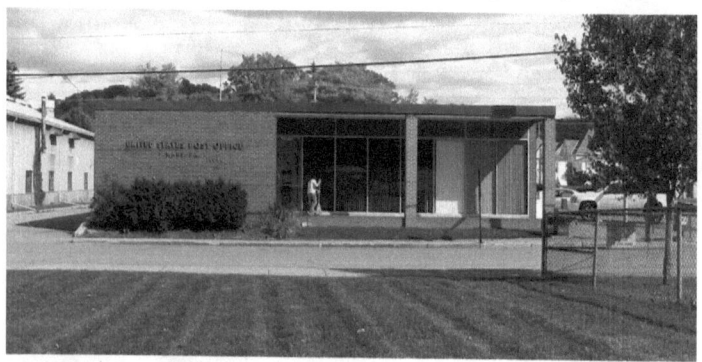

A woman with a broom comes out the door. She sweeps the fine dust of Mars across the floor and then picks up an unidentified object. She lifts the lid of a trash bin, puts the object in, closes the lid, brushes the dust across the window sill, walks back to the door and does a couple of random strokes in the immediate entrance area. She reenters the post office and while the glass door behind her is closing, a man talking into a voice transmitter walks towards the entrance rather swiftly. He opens the door with his left hand, walks in and three seconds later we see him again, as he opens the next door inside the post office that leads from the lobby into the main chamber. A white surface rover pulls up on the curb and a woman walks around the side of the building. She has straight, blond hair and wears an absorbing brown jacket over a long pink T-shirt and a patted bra. She enters the building and while the glass door behind her is closing the white surface rover on the curb leaves its spot and starts driving down the dust sealed surface. This is life in Mars.

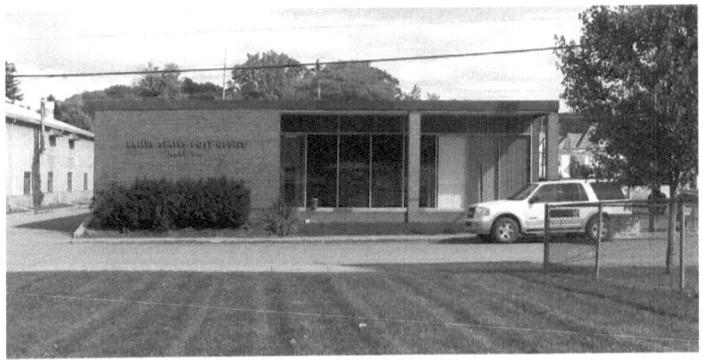

We get back into the Chrysler and decide to leave the center and drive further out into the heartland. The first development, Heritage Creek, which we reach 10 minutes later, glows yellow atop a freshly dumped mountain of brown dirt. The village is only partially realized. There are some weeds in the foreground, willingly cooperating with the randomized flows of solar wind.

They are backed by a row of small firs the developers have planted in their foresight. Not long from now, the firs will be the only plants around the settlement. The wild flowers and weeds will be gone, replaced by short, kept, English lawn, and the firs will turn themselves into a natural screen, hiding what's happening behind them, none of it yet in existence, but all of it already sold. We drive up Comfort Lane, we are on the side that's leading in. It's the black lane, the one that's clean, the one that goes up the hill and brings us directly to the metal sales container and the No Trespassing sign. We stop for a while and watch the activities. There is a dump truck patiently standing next to a backhoe that shovels dirt into its bed. There is a patch of grey sidewalk that starts and ends in mud. There is a house on the edge of an artificial cliff, grey and alone, isolated and exposed by repeating patches of blue sky. The chronicles said that 13 years earlier, on a day in August 1999, when the second expedition had landed here, the sky had also been blue, and the sky had also been immense. But 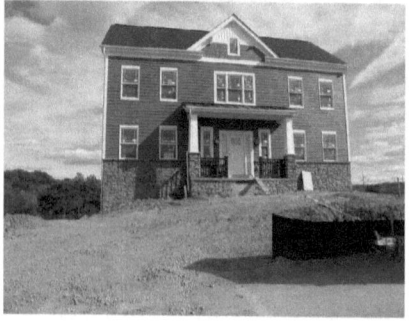 the house knows nothing of the landing. The house is not intelligent, it has no memory. It is nothing but an impression, an impression of home, and as such it simply impresses and

34

we find ourselves wanting to hang onto an artificial cliff like that in a house like that with a nice balcony. We would possibly do it for the boy's childhood, if we could. But we can't.

We slip by the No Trespassing sign and turn into the final stretch of the dead-end road that has been paved into the terra-formed surface of Heritage Creek. We pass by two, and stop at a third construction site. The ground is trembling like a cheap popcorn machine from a run down circus. We lower the windows of our car to hear if there is a reason for that, besides the big generator that powers a cement mixer. A Johnny Cash song is playing somewhere on a radio. *I hurt myself today, to see if I still feel...* Every time Johnny's broken hand strokes the guitar the workmen closest to us shoots another nail into the white plastic foil that covers the wooden structure of a casket, wide enough

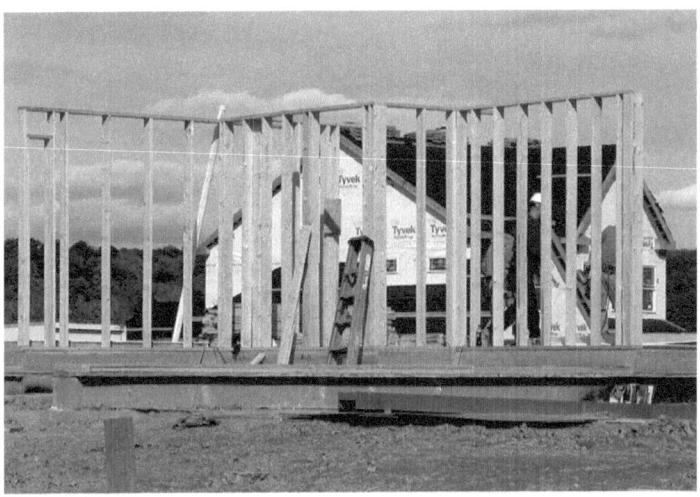

for two family cars. We feel for the wood. We feel for the plastic, we feel for the garage, we even feel for the cars that will rest in there. The pain is real and Johnny Cash is right. Nothing else is.

The men are dusty. They are all wearing heavy belts and plastic helmets. One of them activates the background by carrying light blue sheets of styrofoam across the sandy plain; every time the wind gets hold of the blue surface, the sheet turns into a sail and the man into an aimless drifter.

No one asks us a question. Why would they? It's obvious. There is a man behind the wheel of a brand-new full-size silver Chrysler, there is a woman in the seat right next to him and in the back, strapped into his car seat, the fortunate child. We must be them, the fam-

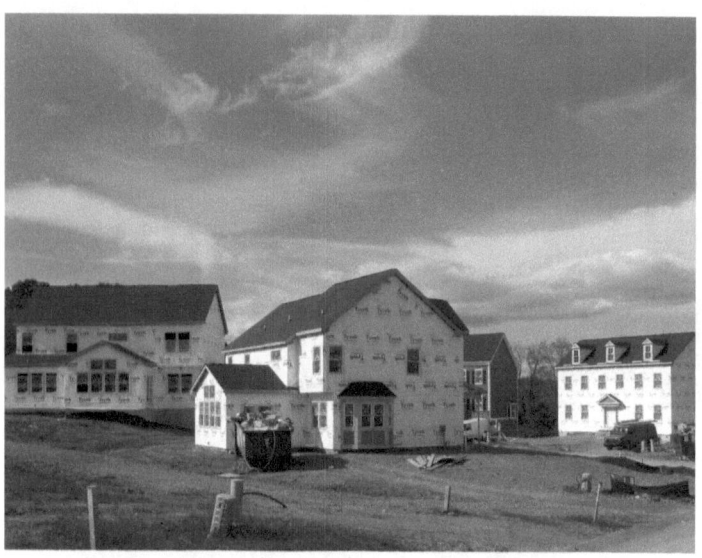

ily who came by in the golden light of the afternoon to watch the construction of their investment in the future. We want to make contact. We get out of the car and approach one of the workers. He asks us what we want. We don't know. He is holding a mask in his hand. We ask him to put it over his face. He takes a dirty sock with a big hole out of the pocket of his fire proof jacket, and pulls this over his face. Then he puts on the grey gas mask and tightens the rubber bands. What's left of his face are two brown pupils that stare at us. We don't know what to say. He gestures something with his red, raw hands, but we don't understand what it could mean. Centuries of failed communication technology fly by, while Johnny Cash keeps playing his tune.

> *If I could start again,*
> *A million miles away*
> *I would keep myself*
> *I would find a way*

We get back into the car and drive down the exit lane, the dirty one covered with mud and the footprints of oversized wheels. The sunshine is gone and the evaporating toxins of the black plastic parts in the vehicle start taking their toll. We have a headache. The child, strapped in the backseat for hours, throws a tantrum. He wants to get out, but there is no outside of this.

> Suppose all of these houses aren't real at all, this bed not real, but only figments of my own imagination, given substance by telepathy and hypnosis through the Martians, thought Captain John Black. Suppose these houses are really some *other* shape, a Martian shape, but, by playing on my desires and wants, these Martians have made this seem like my old home town, my old house, to lull me out of my suspicions.

We turn on the audio system and insert the chip card with the recording of our session with Irene. Her voice is smooth and synchronizes perfectly with the fleeting visuals in front of the windshield, while our voice sounds as flat and distant as the village life that is supposed to happen all around us: "Each section of the developments is divided into small lots," Irene says.

"Some are sold, others are up for sale. I am hearing they are old battlefields."

"What kind of a person would choose a site like this for a future home," we ask her.

She is breathing in. She is breathing out.

"You are asking as if I was an eyewitness to this. But this is not how it works. This landscape is too far away to be seen. You need to change your view, close your eyes and switch into another perspective in time. If you keep your eyes open, Irene continues, you will see Mars as a fabrication. You will see the fabricators with their beefy leather belts. They are covered with dust but in your eyes it's ash, burned particles.

Their intelligence is protected by colored plastic hats, and to you that will be an inappropriate detail, because you will see the construction of our Martian villages as funeral ceremonies. They will be playing a Johnny Cash song, and every time a framer shoots another nail into the white plastic foil that covers the wooden structure of the big casket you will cringe."

We take a deep breath and close our eyes.

"Good," Irene says. "Keep driving. Now stop imagining things. If you keep on imagining things, you will imagine Mars as the place where people will retire from life on Earth. You'll see houses and imagine, that they are inhabited by absentees. Mars will look like a lifeless place. The big houses will look like mausoleums, the small ones like tombs. The villages will look like cemeteries, their own future buried within itself. If you keep imagining, while you are driving around in your silver Chrysler, you inevitably will picture yourself within this setting and you will think how ridiculous it is, to keep driving through these ridiculously ruinous places in a silver rental car. You will think of these ruins as hollow containers that accommodate every possible ruin. The financial ruin, the ecological ruin, the social ruin, the spiritual ruin, the ruined remains of humankind. These ruins hold everything. They even embody the romantic part of you that loves ruins, that respects the idealistic sincerity of ruins, that relishes the pointless stabilization of decay. Your memory relies on ruins. I am being told, that everybody wants to last."

We take a deep breath and stop imagining things.

"Good," Irene says. "Very good. Now stop breathing." We squint, just to get an idea of where this is going. We are in Irene's basement office of the Mars Professional Building. Irene's eyes are still closed, her arms are extended, but she is not wearing the white shirt anymore. We are confused, but it does not matter. We trust her. While what she is saying is distressing, the way she is saying it feels comforting. We close our eyes again. This is the most unassuming nightmare we ever had, and it keeps pulling us in. We keep driving, from one modern day Pleasantville to the next. Each one looks a little different. We enjoy the variety. Roman mansions with an acre of green lawn around them, Victorian style manor houses, Mediterranean villages, Gothic mini-castles, cathedrals and chalets, medieval Tudor structures, ranches, rows of shotgun houses, custom-made cottages, concrete driveways, cobblestone crosswalks and carriage style garage doors, picturesque city lamp posts and every other architectural detail that looks beautiful behind neatly trimmed evergreen bushes. "Keep driving," Irene says. "Keep driving."

After three days, we are done. We conclude the tour in an ice cream shop in a mini mall at the bottom of the hills of Seaton Crest, that offers 20 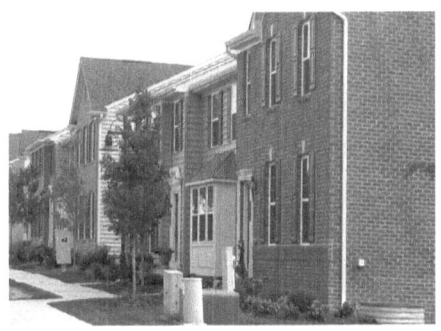 flavors of soft serve, 40 kinds of sprinkles, 26 kinds of sauce and 3 ways to pay to people who otherwise don't like to mix.

We think of the women in the bakery. It's hard to make a decision. On the other hand it's easy, because it's all the same. We self-serve soft mango, vanilla and hazelnut ice cream in a plastic bowl, sprinkle it with crushed peanuts, caramel chunks, coconut flakes and slivered chocolate, and add artificial fruit balls that look like a lion-fish caviar. There are sauces as well, so we add chocolate, strawberry, and vanilla creamer on top. We pay with credit card and then we return to Moon for one last night.

By now are used to the motel. We have even started to like it. Our room, #249, has become a place to return to, and we appreciate the fact that the mountain of chaos we leave in the morning has always been flattened out when we get back. Everything in the room has a patina. The nightstand is scratched and the drawer is wounded, the mirror chipped off, the door has been kicked. There is rust on the faucet but no holes in the walls and no puddles on the floor, and the bathroom door doesn't hang on the frame like a dead fly on a brown glue strip. The room has been through a lot and it survived. What better way to emanate hope.

This is our last night here. We are hungry, but there is no food in Moon except potato chips in aluminum bags. We are thirsty, but there is no place to get a drink, unless we want to slurp a diet soda from a can at the gas station. Besides, there is the little boy, whose precious sleep needs to be guarded. We turn off the light, lie down on the bed and look out the window into the big collective shadow we cast. Moon is a reflection in the dark that shines onto the worn-out grey carpet as if replicating its own surface right in front of us. We are in Moon looking at Moon with open eyes. At least Moon is close enough to be an eyewitness, we think, but the thought has no effect on us. What's the difference between Mars and Moon, we had wondered, when we first came here. Mars is new, and Moon is old. We've been there, we've done that, they say. Moon has served its purpose in a race where ancient nations battled over the privilege to stick their flags into the ground first. But even this first gesture was a fake. There is no wind on moon. The flag was propped up, made to look as if it were waving in the wind. Moon has no atmosphere, no rain, no seasons, and nothing changes there in a million years. It's really not that interesting. Buzz Aldrin once said in an interview that the most unattractive portion of the first moon landing was the return to Earth.

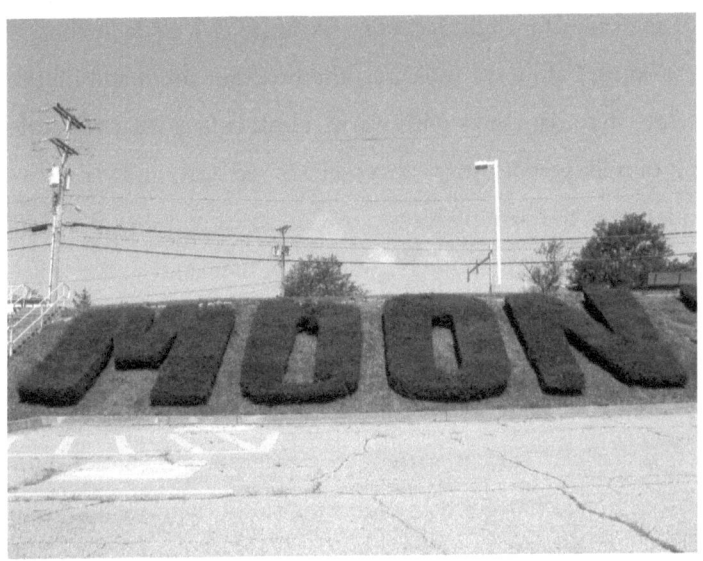

At the 40th anniversary of the Apollo 11 mission, NASA discovered that they had erased the original magnetic tapes of the first moon landing. In the 80s, new satellites had gone up, and were producing a lot of data that needed to be recorded, seven days a week, 24 hours a day, and the agency was experiencing a critical shortage of magnetic tapes. So NASA started erasing old ones and reusing them. No one even noticed for 35 years. These are the simple tales of an undeniable truth. Moon is there, that's all. Moon is like our motel room at the America's Best Value Inn— the most common place on Earth, where you know you can return as a last resort and they have to take you in.

We keep quietly rotating for eight hours, and wake up at 7am when the dark of the night has been replaced by a view of the sun. Our flight leaves in six hours. We smile at the receptionist before we walk into the breakfast room and fill the white styrofoam cups with warm, bleak coffee. We add a little bit of milk powder, stir with a piece of red straw and walk outside across the parking lot towards the satellite dishes. We place the coffee cups inside the biggest one of them and let the coffee microwave for a while. The antenna in the center of the dish points in the direction of the airport, where a plane is landing or taking off every two minutes with a loud roar. People arrive on aircraft and leave in cars, or they arrive in cars and leave inside an aircraft. More than eight million of them each year. In just a couple of hours we'll submit our bodies into that system. We check the time. It's 7:49am. We take the coffee out of the satellite dish, get into the car, and drive to Mars. When we sit down on the waiting bench in the barbershop 40 minutes later, we still have three sips of coffee and some sugar left to fully wake up. It's cozy in there. The radio station plays romantic classics and the customers on the chairs look as relaxed as a bunch of gutted herrings in a bucket. The brother is in, running the electric razor smoothly around a young man's skull. He is tall and handsome enough to be a cowboy in an Italian western, who makes himself understood by the way he lifts or drops the corner of his mouth.

People come, people go. They are mostly male, unless they are under eighteen and need a mother to drive them around. The barber with the Three Stooges tie finds that detail so funny that he keeps laughing about it. Next to the bottles of hairspray, aftershave, shaving cream, water and whiskey, a pair of scissors, a brush, three booster seats, a broom and his electrical razor, which he uses as props, he has a whole trunk of routines up his white-ironed sleeves. Every cape-covered costumer gives him a chance to practice. If the man is old enough, the comedian starts talking about the bold patches on the head as if it they were on a baseball field: "Let's see. You want to learn the names of the players? We have who's on first, what's on second, I don't know's on third," and so on. If the man is middle-aged, he says: "What's the difference between a girlfriend and a wife? And if the boy is under sixteen he asks: "What do you call an ant that skips school?" And no matter where the routine goes from there, it culminates with: "Tell them where you got it," referring to yet another buzz cut he has mastered in the preceding 15 minutes as a byproduct, while heartily shaking their hands.

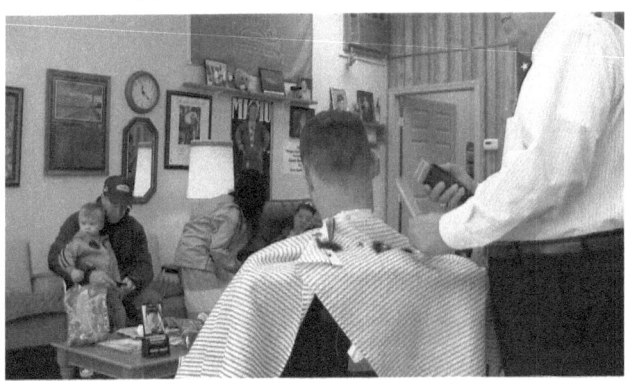

Elvis comes on the radio. The cowboy starts tapping his foot.

Baby let me be, your lovin' teddy bear
Put a chain around my neck, and lead me anywhere
Oh let me be your teddy bear

I remember that song, the comedian says. It was the number one hit during the summer of 1957, and it stayed number one for the whole summer. "Remember Julie, Anthony?" He grins in his brother's direction, swings his big hips and starts singing along:

I don't wanna be a tiger, cause tigers play too rough
I don't wanna be a lion, cause lions ain't the kind you love enough

When the song is finished, another round of costumers has left the shop. The cowboy barber gives us a couple minutes of extra time on the waiting bench and then he talks to us: "We are strangers in this place— just like you." We think about his words. The statement might rightly refer to the fact that we originated in the same region of coordinates, but otherwise it's nothing but a lie that makes us feel good. This cowboy is no stranger. He might be as uncertain about his place in time as everybody else in Mars, or Moon or Venus, but at least he knows enough to get him through the days as a human be-ing, capable of talking with others. He knows the first and last names of each of his customers. He knows how hard they press when they shake hands, he knows the license plate numbers of their cars, he knows how much gas they have in the tank and when their wives are having their periods, if they are still having them. He knows how many stitches were needed to close the bleeding wounds of the men in Mars, and he knows what's wrong with their inner organs. And he knows that everyone who comes to him cleans their ears before they get a haircut, otherwise he sends them home. He has stuff to talk about.

We, on the other hand, know nothing about this place and we don't have time to get to know it, either. Hurricane Sandy will hit in less than a week, and the end of the world on 12/21/2012 is not even two months away. We are in a rush and have practically no other option but to forecast the future as a fossil, an imprint of an already-extinct fern. Mars will survive because it's already dead.

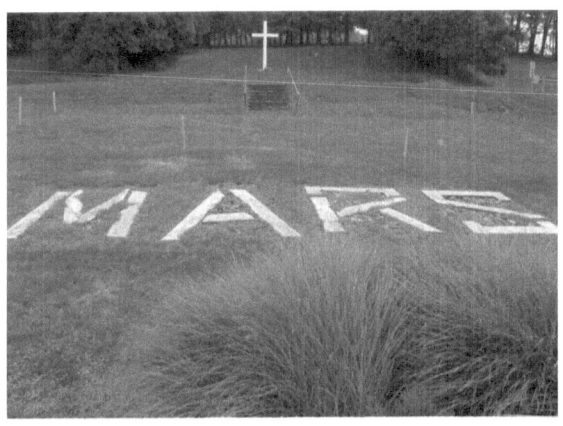

The cowboy barber comes over to the waiting bench and gives our little boy another present and says: "For my little girl." "He is a boy," we tell him - like we did when he gave him a stuffed monkey in a baseball uniform that someone had donated for a cancer fundraiser, and when he rubbed an "I Love America" tattoo on his arm. The cowboy ignores our correction again and we realize that this is his way of letting us know that long hair like this on a boy is impossible. "There are telling me…" Irene had said when we asked her about Mars as an option for life beyond Earth, "that the schools are very good here, the child would go to a very good school … but they also like me to tell you … that the quirky don't quite fit in…"

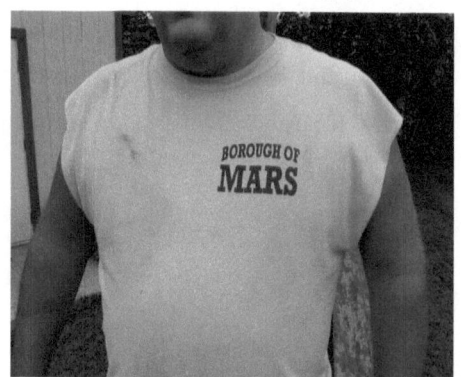

Outside, across the street, perfectly framed by the big windows of the shop, appears a father with two boys and a girl in a MARS cheerleader uniform. The comedian turns everybody's attention towards the group. "There is no way to prevent it," he cries, as they approach the glass door like a landslide. The door opens, the bell rings, and while the father and the children are entering the comedian throws his arms into the air, as if he were about to do a backwards flip from the ten-foot-high diving board at the Mars Pool: "Every Saturday we start out as a barber shop. Then guys like you show up and make us look like a daycare." The father looks confused. "It says 'Walk-In' on the window," he offers, as an apology. The comedian doesn't respond. He turns his back towards the under-aged and shovels through the drawer where everybody in Mars keeps their personal stuff; papers with phone numbers and rubber bands, nail clippers and pens, temporary tattoos, business cards, and dollar bills. Nobody says a word. The comedian lets the father's helplessness last, edging him towards the point of admitting that having three kids is having a few too many. He breaks the tension just before it turns awkward. He orders the children to sit down, like chickens in a row, and forbids them to lay any eggs. He says to the father: "Here is a fifty. Go across the street and tell the woman in the bank that Vincent needs singles, will ya?" The father looks startled, but when his searching eyes meet the piercing eyes of the cowboy brother he takes the fifty, and walks straight out onto the street without another look at the three children he leaves behind. The comedian assesses the abandoned brood and congratulates them on being so well-behaved. He starts piling up black booster seats on his chair, first two and then three on top of each other and then it's our turn to put the smallest one of the kids, a two-year-old boy, atop the tower to meet the king of buzz cuts.

Like the heads of everyone before him the little boy's top

part gets separated by the neck from the rest of the universe as the comedian clips the barber cape on, and then the magic starts. The scissors turn into the beak of a big, chippy-chappy bird, the razor is a choo-choo train that commutes between left and right ear, and then water drippy droppy rains out of a spray bottle. This is followed by some kind of "Oh nooo!" atomic disaster, whereupon the barber switches into a double role, pressing the thumb of his right hand on the top of an industrial-sized can of hairspray to simulate radioactive fall-out, while using the back of his left hand to protect the little boy from turning blind. Everybody loves the show, especially the little boy, and when the father returns from his mission to the bank with a stack of fifty singles, he is greeted by a young, cheerful creature, who looks like he could serve the nation as a future soldier in a future army. "Did I actually say he need-ed a haircut?" the father inquires, now even more confused. The comedian looks at the cowboy. "Welcome to Mars," the cowboy says, and walks towards the man like an older broth-er after his younger brother has been challenged on the play-ground. "Are you new to this place?" he asks, and extends his hand to administer a forgiving handshake, while the comedian turns around and takes a sip out of his whiskey bottle. "My name is Anthony," the cowboy says to the father. "And this…", he says, leaving enough time between the words so that his brother can put the bottle back into the bottom drawer without the children seeing it, "is my brother Vincent. We've been running this business here since 1969. What's your name?"

"Frank. My name is Frank."

"What are the names of the children?"

"The little one is Sam, the older one is Jason, and the girl is Megan."

"You moved here?"

"Yes, we bought a house in Trotting Acres."

"What street is it on?"

"It's on Smallwood Drive."

"The grey one with the aluminum door?"

"Yes."

"That's a beautiful house. Have a seat, sir. What can I do for you?"

"Just the usual."

This is the heart of Mars. We have found the mothership. This is the place where the last manned mission touched down, where the remains are kept alive, where the heart they rescued with the rocket ship keeps beating. They are no barbers. They are astronauts, they are Neil Armstrong and Buzz Aldrin. They accomplished the mission, they landed, they left the rocket ship, but leaving the first footprints can only be done once, while getting a haircut is always in demand. And so what else is there to do, but run the barber shop like an undercover recharge station for humanity, supplying little doses of earthly decency for the Martians to get a taste. They've driven the concept to perfection. They have the mix that everybody loves, of all the things that nobody really likes. They have the teddy bear for the kids, they have the plastic flowers for the ladies, they have green foam cushions for the waiting bench, and they have the "Walk Ins Welcome" sign on the door. They have a jar for the breast cancer fundraiser, they have a jar for lollipops, they have pictures of grandchildren sitting on the laps of Santa Clauses next to erotic magazine clippings of celebrities in miniskirts, soldiers in uniform and waterfalls in paradise. They have a bible in a drawer and a small gun in the other, they have the oversized American flag on the wall and they have Andy Williams, the king of easy, on the radio, who steps up to the moment and delivers "Moon River" in the most decent, even-tempered, thoroughly relaxing way.

Moon river, wider than a mile, I'm crossing you in style someday
Oh, dream-maker, you heart-breaker,
Wherever you're goin', I'm goin' your way...

Nobody speaks anymore. Everyone just keeps going on in silence. The cars keep passing by outside the window, and the wind keeps blowing the last leaves down the sidewalk. The barbers keep cutting hair. The blond man in front of the comedian, a middle-aged bachelor with a big bald spot, has closed his eyes, and smiles as if he is having a little dream. The father in front of the cowboy gently rocks his youngest on his knees and stares at the layer of transparent air in front of him. His other two children are swinging back and forth in the big brown rocking chair.

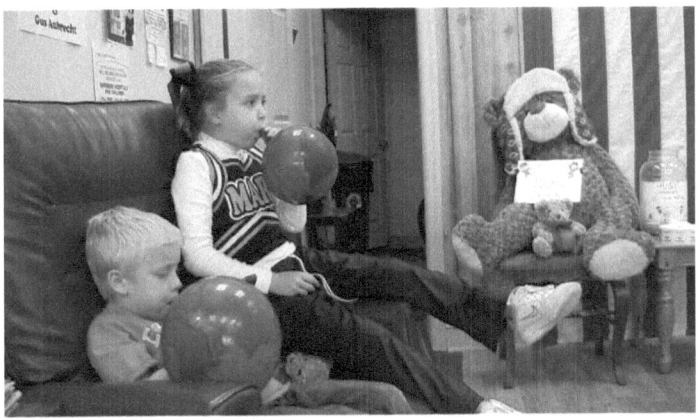

They are blowing up blue balloons with seven green continents printed on them. Each time they go forward they exhale into the rubber bubble and blow it up, and when they rock back they inhale the content, so the bubble deflates. It's all the same air and they keep inhaling it over and over again without fainting.

Two drifters, off to see the world
There's such a lot of world to see
We're after the same rainbow's end, waitin' 'round the bend
My huckleberry friend, moon river, and me
Two drifters, off to see the world
There's such a lot of world to see…

That's it. That's the sign! The earth is a balloon, inflating and deflating; that's what's causing the weather to change, what's causing the tides to occur and the oceans to surge. Mars isn't supposed to forecast anything. We are not ready yet. "The vibration is just not there yet," Irene had said. "It's only 2012. I am getting something along the lines of 2030."

> *Two drifters, off to see the world*
> *There's such a lot of world to see*
> *We're after the same rainbow's end, waitin' 'round the bend*
> *My huckleberry friend, moon river, and me*

The comedian is cleaning the bachelor's neck with a brush, the brave little soldier is unwrapping another candy, and our beautiful gender-unspecific creature keeps sucking dreamily on his third, red lollipop. It's not even noon, but the day feels so unlikely already that the sentimental one of us gets teary from the music. The tough guy knows. He smiles at his brother and throws a nod into our direction. The comedian takes the cape off the bachelor, pats the bold spot for a little while to wake him up, and then comes over to the waiting bench.

"He didn't want us to feel badly. He told us it would happen one day and he didn't want us to cry. He didn't teach us how, you know. He didn't want us to know.

He gives us a hug, whispers: "We love you," and then he throws everybody out. We follow the father and the children around the building to the village green. The girl climbs on the silver saucer. Once she stands on top of the antenna, freely with nothing else to grab onto but the blue earth balloon, she calls out: "Come on board".

Her two brothers and our boy are starting to climb up and once they sit on the platform, they all shout:

"Come on board!"

"You guys go ahead," the father says.

"We'll stay in Mars."

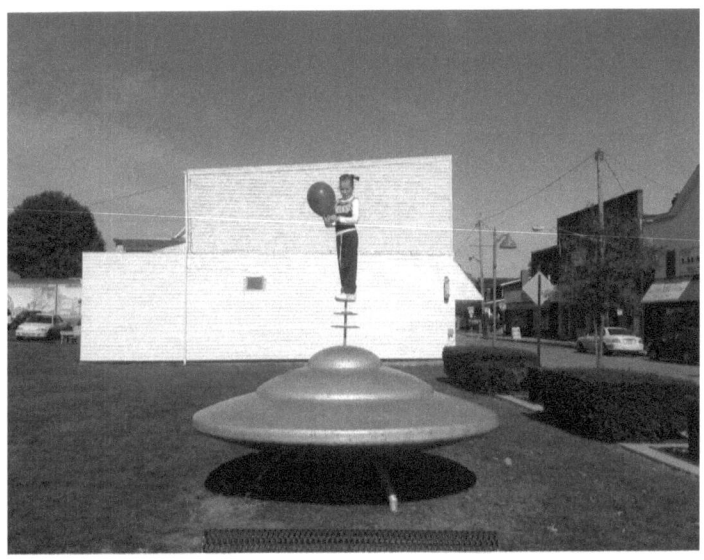

Quotes: The Martian Chronicles, by Ray Bradbury, originally
puplished in 1950 by Doubleday Publishers, NYC
Editor: Will Brand
Design: eteam
Photograph on page 27 by Vik Nanda
Book Cover on page 15: 1979 Bantam Books paperback
edition, illustrated by Ian Miller
all other photographs: eteam

Special Thanks to:
Calcara's Barber Styling Shop, Renee Takacs,
Mars Historical Society and Tyler Stallings

Further information: www.meineigenheim.org